Meat- Eating eye view Plants

by Penny Harwood

WATERBIRD BOOKS

Columbus, Ohio

Mc Graw Hill **Children's Publishing**

This edition published in the United States of America in 2003 by
Waterbird Books
an imprint of McGraw-Hill Children's Publishing,
a Division of The McGraw-Hill Companies
8787 Orion Place
Columbus, Ohio 43240-4027

www.MHkids.com

Library of Congress Cataloging-in-Publication Data is on file with the publisher.

First published in Great Britain in 2002 by ticktock Media Ltd.,
Unit 2 Orchard Business Centre, North Farm Road, Tunbridge Wells, Kent TN3 3XF.
Photography by Roddy Paine Photographic Studios. Illustrations by Simon Clare Creative Workshop
Text and illustrations © 2002 ticktock Entertainment Ltd.

Printed in Hong Kong.

1-57768-565-2

1 2 3 4 5 6 7 8 9 10 TTM 09 08 07 06 05 04 03

Contents

All words appearing in the text in bold, **like this**, are explained in the glossary.

Think...

Do they have mouths?

How do they trap their **prey**?

How do they eat?

All plants need light from the sun, water from the soil, and carbon dioxide from the air in order to grow. But some plants grow in places with poor soil—in deserts, on mountainsides, or even on the branches of rain forest trees. These plants supplement their diets with juicy, **nutrient**-rich bugs! They actually eat meat! These plants are called *carnivorous plants*.

4

Imagine...

If you were a bug, would you fall into their **trap**?

It looks like you are about to find out...

Aaghhh...

This is a pitcher plant.

Pitcher plants grow in the **bogs** and swamps of the United States. They are sometimes called North American pitcher plants.

The inside of the pitcher plant is very slippery. Any bug that climbs in will lose its grip on the surface and slide down!

Can you see the tiny **hairs** that grow on the lid of the plant? They help the bugs hang on—briefly!

Bugs are attracted to the bright colors and sugary on the lid of the plant.

I'm going to fall!

Pitchers sleep during the winter when there are no bugs to eat. They turn brown and wither, turning green again in the spring.

These plants have **digestive juices** (like you have in your stomach) at the bottom of their long stems. When a bug falls down into the juice, it dissolves. Its **nutrients** are soaked up by the plant.

This is a Venus's flytrap.

Venus's flytraps are the best-known carnivorous plants. Like some other meat-eating plants, they actually move to catch their prey.

The bright color of the Venus's flytrap's mouth lures bugs inside.

There are tiny hairs on the inside of the plant's mouth. The slightest touch of these hairs will cause the trap to shut.

Traps die after they have closed three times. If a trap is cut off, though, it will regrow.

The **teeth** on the edge of the trap close so tightly that a bug cannot break free.

When the trap is shut, the plant releases its digestive juices and absorbs all the nutrients from the bug, leaving just a dry shell.

9

Aaghh!

Is this a snake?

11

The trapped bug flies at the windows again and again, soon becoming confused.

Once inside, a fringe of hairs forces the bug toward the back of the trap, where the surface is dangerously slippery.

Waiting for the bug at the bottom of the neck is a pool of water and digestive juices.

12

No, it's a cobra lily.

These plants look like cobra snakes
and are just as deadly
to bugs!

Cobra lilies can live
in mountain bogs as
high up as 8,000
feet!

Their fanglike
leaves act as
landing pads
for bugs, which
are attracted
to the bright
pink color and
sweet taste.
Once the bug
lands, it soon
enters the trap.

This is a sun pitcher.

It is only found in South America. This plant has a spoon-shaped leaf with nectar inside.

Bugs lose their balance on the slippery nectar of the spoon and fall down through the plant.

It's like falling down a well!

The sun pitcher eats the trapped bugs by attacking them with **bacteria**.

The red coloring on a sun pitcher increases when the plant gets a lot of sunlight.

This plant is bright and sugary—good enough to eat!

Each horn is really a leaf that has wrapped around and joined together to make a trap for unsuspecting bugs!

Is this a monster

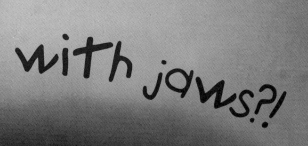

with jaws?!

17

No it's just a small Albany pitcher.

Albany pitchers are found in wet, grassy areas of Australia.

The lid of the trap

The sharp teeth surround the opening of the trap, making it impossible for a bug to escape after it has fallen in!

Once a bug is inside the trap, it loses its grip on the surface and falls into a pool of digestive juices.

Albany pitchers have hairs on the outside of the trap. They are used to guide bugs inside where they will be attracted by the nectar on the walls.

The Albany pitcher's traps look a little like baby booties.

The lid of the trap can close to protect the digestive juices from drying up in hot weather.

Albany pitchers are not very big. They grow to a maximum of $1\frac{1}{2}$ inches in length.

This is a monkey cup.

Monkey cups grow on trees in the tropical rain forests of southeast Asia.

Each cup has special areas around the lid that give off nectar, attracting bugs and sometimes small animals, too.

Bugs are also attracted to the bright pink color of the lid.

Bugs and other tiny creatures fall down into the cup and are dissolved by the digestive juices at the bottom.

The monkey cups are really the plant's traps, but like most carnivorous plants, these traps don't actually close.

These spikes along the side of the monkey cup also help trap bugs.

Monkeys have been seen using the cups to drink from!

YIKES!
It's like a jungle in here!

The **tentacles** on the sundew's leaves are covered with drops of sticky fluid.

The fluid glistens and sparkles in the sun. It looks just like dew. But when bugs land on the tentacles, they get stuck!

Sundews are lovely to look at and are attractive to bugs, but they should watch out— once in its clutches, there's no escape!

The bug struggles, but that only traps it more!

It's a sundew jungle.

There are many different types of sundew. They can grow in very cold places like Siberia and very hot countries like Brazil.

The leaf curls around the bug

to make sure it can't escape.

The sundew releases **proteins** through its tentacles. These dissolve the trapped bug so the plant can digest it.

25

This is a butterwort.

Can you see the tiny tentacles on the leaves?

The tentacles produce a gluey fluid. This makes the leaves feel like butter when you touch them.

A butterwort's flower can be pink, violet, or red.

Bugs are attracted to the beautiful flower.

Butterworts love to grow in mossy, mountainous places and boggy, wet places. Sometimes they even grow on trees.

The leaves of the butterwort smell musty, a bit like mushrooms. This smell also attracts bugs.

This butterwort is from Ireland.

The bug sticks to the fluid on the butterwort's leaves. Then it is slowly dissolved and absorbed by the plant.

27

This is a bladderwort.

The stem of the bladderwort can grow up to ten feet high (as tall as an African elephant)!

Bladderworts attract bugs with their flowers.

The trap is called a bladder. Each one is less than 1/16 of an inch wide.

Bladderworts probably have the most complicated trap of all carnivorous plants, and possibly the tiniest. They are hidden, sometimes underground or underwater!

The bladder has a trap door that opens when a bug touches one of the two or three trigger hairs on the outside.

When a bug touches the trigger hairs, the bladder sucks them in like a vacuum cleaner, along with a small amount of water. The bladder then releases the water, but not the bug!

The traps are down here!

GLOSSARY

BACTERIA Group of tiny, microscopic organisms that live in soil, water, or inside plants and animals. They cause chemical reactions that help plants and animals digest their food.

BOG An area of wet, spongy ground.

DIGESTIVE JUICES Liquid inside an animal or plant that it uses to turn food into a form it can use.

HAIRS Threadlike growths on the surface of a plant or animal.

LEAVES Flat outgrowths on a plant's stems used to collect sunlight.

NECTAR Sweet liquid produced by plants. It is gathered by bees and made into honey.

NUTRIENTS The goodness in the bugs that the plants need to help them grow.

PREY An animal caught as food by another animal or plant.

PROTEIN Natural chemical found in plant and animal cells.

TEETH Hard, bony structures on plants that resemble the teeth of animals.

TENTACLES Very long and very flexible hairs of an animal or plant.

TRAPS Devices used by plants to catch insects.

INDEX